BASIC ILLUSTRATED
Backpacking

Harry Roberts
Revised by Russ Schneider

Illustrations by Lon Levin

FALCONGUIDES ®

GUILFORD, CONNECTICUT
HELENA, MONTANA
AN IMPRINT OF THE GLOBE PEQUOT PRESS

FALCONGUIDES®

Copyright © 2008 Morris Book Publishing, LLC

Text and page design by Karen Williams [intudesign.net]
Photos pages 1, 9, and 47 © Photodisc; pages 16, 18, 23, 33, and 39 © istockphoto.

Library of Congress Cataloging-in-Publication Data is available.

ISBN 978-0-7627-4757-3

Printed in China
First Edition/First Printing

Contents

Introduction

It's always struck me as strange to start a book on any activity, be it gourmet cooking or model railroading, with a long, passionate bleat about how much FUN it is. It'd seem only reasonable to assume that you, the reader, bought the book in the first place to read about something that you already figured would be fun. I mean, when was the last time you bought a book about hitting your thumb with a clawhammer?

Agreed, then . . . backpacking and its less strenuous cousin, walking in the woods, are fun. My job here is not to tell you that it's fun. It's to show you how to do some things when you're out there that'll *keep* it fun for you, your family, and your friends.

Let's run through that last sentence again. My job is to show you how to do some things. My job is not to tell you to buy some things. You'll need some gear, no doubt. And you may need some words of common-sense advice about choosing gear. But I've always felt that if you understand the demands placed on equipment and how to use that equipment, you can make informed decisions for yourself. The most expensive gear in the outdoor sports shop is most frequently the best gear available; this is still an honest game, in which you get what you pay for. But you'll still sleep cold in your top-of-the-line down bag if you don't know how to sleep in a sleeping bag. And I don't care how light each one of those wonderful little gadgets is that you're carrying around to make your life comfortable out there. They still have to be carried around on your back, and your back can't tell the difference between 30 extra pounds of the best superlight toys and 30 pounds of bricks.

Don't get me wrong. I like toys; I like neat things that work. But all the neat toys in the store won't keep you as warm, dry, and generally comfortable as will a few ounces of knowledge.

That's my sermon for today. Let's take a walk in the woods!

Getting Started

If you think of it as "backpacking," your head will be screwed on wrong from the start, because backpacking has had a wealth of connotations grow up about it that have no place in the real world out there.

When you take a walk in the woods for a day, you take some of your closet and some of the kitchen with you. When you take a walk in the woods for more than a day, you have to take the bedroom with you and a little more of the kitchen. That's it. All backpacking is, in terms of gear, is dayhiking with a bedroom. This cuts away a lot of precious nonsense and also leaves you receptive to some ideas about straightforward, functional gear selection and use.

You start in backpacking by taking a walk in the woods. After a lot of walks in the woods, you start to get very comfortable out there, and you almost resent walking back out to your car. You'd like to stay the night, so you can see more and be out there longer. Then and only then is when you consider backpacking.

Until that time you're just taking walks in the woods. You can glorify those walks by telling your friends that you're going hiking, but there are few uglier words than "hiking" in the English language. "Hiking" is what you do with a field pack and an assault rifle in a swamp in South Carolina. "Hiking" is what you did as a twelve year old when you refused to believe that you could survive a night in the woods without a portable radio, five changes of clothing, 4 pounds of Oreos, a 12-inch cast iron frypan, an 11-pound sleeping bag, and three 40-ounce bottles of cola. "Hiking" is what you do when the manager comes to the mound and asks for the ball because you've just given up six straight extra-base hits. "Take a hike, son." Sure.

You can take a hike if you wish. I'll take a walk in the woods.

And any woods will do.

In fact, you don't even need woods. Open country's just fine. It doesn't have to be in the Smokies or the Ozarks or the Sierras or the Adirondacks or the Rockies. It doesn't have to be famous or glamorous or written about in ecosport magazines. It simply has to be there, be close by, and be public. This may seem terribly obvious when it's put down here in plain old black and white, but it isn't obvious to a whole lot of people, who stay indoors and dream about distant vistas when they could be out and about near home.

Don't get seduced by the exotic. Don't dream so much about the Wonderland Trail that circumnavigates Mount Rainier that you forget the wonderland next door.

How to Walk. Huh? "But I know how to walk!" you say. I can't argue with that. But most people, who otherwise walk reasonably well, take some notion of how they should walk with a pack to heart and wind up expending vast amounts of energy with little return for it.

To begin with, the woods walker, with or without a pack, is more often than not on irregular terrain, where balance is a bit more of a problem. Add a pack, and you find that you're simply not quite as catlike in the outback as you are on a gym floor. Rule One? Shorten your stride. Keep your feet under you.

Rule Two? Walk erect. I know; this isn't always easy on a trail. But the more erect you are, the easier it is to carry a load, the more comfortable the pack will be, and the happier your back will be. If you find yourself slumping, carry a staff or a long walking stick. And try this gimmick when you have to go up a sharp little hill or one of those interminable, not-steep-enough-to-rest-on-but-too-steep-for-comfort grinds that takes you up 1,000 feet per mile. Straighten up, shorten your stride, pause for a split second before you push yourself uphill with each stride, and *walk with your hands on your hips*. I've never taken the time to investigate just why this works, but it does. Try it.

And that's it. Go walk somewhere with your house on your back!

Attitudes

Everything you need to know about functioning easily and happily in the outback can be learned with very little difficulty. Being comfortable in good weather and making do in bad is, after all, a game that rewards attention to detail rather than an intelligence rating that qualifies you for Mensa. In short, it's a game that most people can learn.

What is somewhat less predictable is the set of attitudes you bring to the game. It's those attitudes that ultimately determine whether or not you'll enjoy it out there and, more to the point, whether anybody traveling with you will enjoy it.

Start with this. Tattoo it on the back of your right hand if your memory is poor. Just don't forget it.

I am not here to conquer anything.

If you still have room on your hand, put this on it now:

The slowest person in this party is working as hard as I am.

Now put this on the back of your left hand:

A trail is not a combat zone.

Okay. You can go out there now.

CHAPTER 1

First Steps: The ABCs of Trip Planning

There aren't many places in North America that don't have some sort of public parkland nearby. It may be a county park, a state park, a provincial park in Canada, a state forest, a Nature Conservancy area, or even a national park or national forest. Whatever it's called, it's a place to take a walk in the woods.

How do you find places like this?

The easiest way is to get on the Internet. It's a vast and largely free source of local trail information, including aerial photos and printable topographic maps.

For the more personal touch, you can pick up the telephone book, turn to the Yellow Pages, and look under Camping Equipment, Sporting Goods, or Mountain Climbing Equipment, and make a few telephone calls. Discard any shops that answer with something like "Uh, well, hey, nobody walks any more. Wanna buy a four-wheeler cheap?" In time, you'll find a shop that sells hiking and backpacking gear. That's where the inside information is. Go to this store and ask the friendly folks who work there about local public lands. They'll know. They'll also know how to contact the state agency that deals with outdoor recreation, which may have a misleading name like Department of Fish and Wildlife or Department of Environmental Conservation, but which will have, somewhere in its innards, a group that oversees walking, canoeing, and ski-touring trails. It'll probably be called Forest Recreation. It will have some publications and maps available, and it will be under-staffed, so don't expect them to fit boots for you or find you the perfect backcountry hidey-hole.

Your favorite local outdoor outfitter will have detailed maps of pop-ular trails in your area. If you're considering walking a trail in another state or county, check with a local outdoor store for maps and advice. You might find that what looked good on the map sent from the state park doesn't discuss the all-terrain-vehicle trail that runs alongside the "27-mile nature trail." There's nothing worse than traveling 250 miles with the intention of walking into solitude and finding your "nature trail" buzzing with Honda ES 450s tearing through the state forest.

This atrocity can be avoided by a call to a local outfitting store. If no store is in the area, consult the town's bureau of tourism. A well-made map can help; however, even the finest maps will not warn you about a problem like a noisy motorcycle trail.

The Earth Science Information Center (ESIC) will help you find spe-cial purpose maps of all kinds; it is a good source of topographic maps (see Figure 1 for an example). It sorts and collects cartographic

When looking for a place to walk, consult:

- Friends and coworkers
- Local outdoor gear outfitters and staff
- Local hiking and outdoor clubs
- Local conservation organizations
- U.S.D.A. Forest Service, National Park Service, Bureau of Land Management rangers, and visitor center interpretive staff
- The Internet:
  American Hiking Society: www.americanhiking.org
  U.S.D.A. Forest Service: www.fs.fed.us
  National Park Service: www.nps.gov
  FalconGuides: www.falconguides.com
  The National Map (USGS): www.nationalmap.gov
  Trails.com: www.trails.com

EARTH SCIENCE INFORMATION CENTERS (EISC)

1-888-ASK-USGS
www.usgs.gov

Anchorage-ESIC
U.S. Geological Survey
4230 University Drive, Room 101
Anchorage, AK 99508-4664
Telephone: 907-786-7011
Fax: 907-786-7050

Denver-ESIC
U.S. Geological Survey
Box 25286, Building 810
Denver Federal Center
Denver, CO 80225
Telephone: 303-202-4200
Fax: 303-202-4188

Menlo Park-ESIC
U.S. Geological Survey
Building 3, MS 532, Room 3128
345 Middlefield Road
Menlo Park, CA 94025-3591
Telephone: 650-329-4309
Fax: 650-329-5130
wmcesic@usgs.gov

Reston-ESIC
U.S. Geological Survey
507 National Center
Reston, VA 20192
Telephone: 703-648-5953
Fax: 703-648-5548
TDD: 703-648-4119

Rolla-ESIC
U.S. Geological Survey
1400 Independence Road, MS 231
Rolla, MO 65401-2602
Telephone: 573-308-3500
Fax: 573-308-3615

Sioux Falls-ESIC
U.S. Geological Survey
EROS Data Center
Sioux Falls, SD 57198-0001
Telephone: 605-594-6151
Fax: 605-594-6589
TDD: 605-594-6933
custserv@usgs.gov

TOPOGRAPHIC MAP COMPANIES AND ORGANIZATIONS

DeLorme
Two DeLorme Drive
P.O. Box 298
Yarmouth, ME 04096
1-800-561-5105
www.delorme.com

Green Trails, Inc.
P.O. Box 77734
Seattle, WA 98177
206-546-6277
www.greentrails.com

Maptech, Inc.
10 Industrial Way
Amesbury, MA 01913
1-888-839-5551
www.maptech.com

National Geographic Maps
National Geographic/Trails Illustrated
National Geographic/Topo!

P.O. Box 98199
Washington, D.C. 20090-8199
www.nationalgeographic.com/maps

USGS Information Services
(Map and Book Sales)
Box 25286
Denver Federal Center
Denver, CO 80225
Telephone: 303-202-4700
Fax: 303-202-4693

USGS Information Services
(Open-File Report Sales)
Box 25286
Denver Federal Center
Denver, CO 80225
Telephone: 303-202-4700
Fax: 303-202-4188

The National Map (USGS)
www.nationalmap.gov

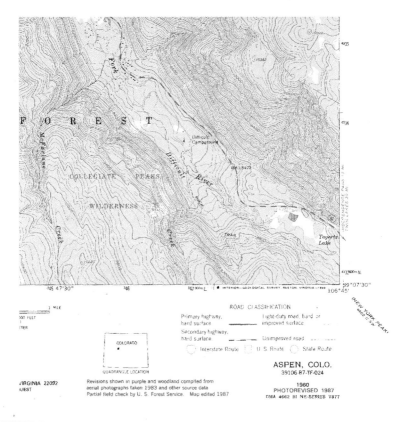

FIGURE 1

A sample topographic map.

information from federal, state, and local government agencies. Contact the ESIC. office nearest you for a listing of city, county, state, and federal area maps and aerial photos. Often, these maps are easily accessed on the Internet. The ESIC will answer all your map questions and sell you what you need. They have a ton of free pamphlets and other information.

Now you're armed with a lot of information about where to go. Some of it looks absolutely compelling. Some of it looks pretty esoteric. Some of it deals with unappetizing places like swamps. In time you'll turn a back somersault and shout "Hallelujah" when you find a new swamp. Right off the bat you'll probably shudder and pass on the wetlands. That's all right. You'll learn.

Now let's go back to those pleasant people who work at the shop that sells backpacking gear and make a few small purchases. If you'll be walking in the woods by yourself, go alone. If you're walking with your family, take your family. I say this as a grizzled veteran spouse, dad, and grandfather. Take the family!

But Where to Walk? Basic Trip Planning

It should be obvious that we're not going to plan your first trip right here. But we're going to talk over a few notions that should make your first trip—and all other trips—easier and more pleasurable for you. Because the "planning" we're talking about here is planning for terrain.

The last time you were at your friendly local outfitter's, you heard some veteran backpackers talking about what they called a neat, easy weekend trip. Hey! Just the thing for you and your spouse and the ten-year-old. So you pick up the trail map (see Figure 2) and the guidebook to the trail systems in the Pellagra State Wilderness, and you charge on home with the good news.

"Yep! Here it is! You start out at the Blackfly Brook parking area, go 11 miles—really only 10.73 miles—across Toothache Ridge and Blister Butte to Dead Hiker Clearing. That's not bad at all. We walked about 12 miles last Saturday, and it was a piece of cake!"

Yep. It was a piece of cake. Flatland walking on old tote roads, carrying a 7-pound daypack. A lovely piece of cake and well within your capacities. The walk to Dead Hiker Clearing might be shorter, but let's look at the guidebook and the map some more.

Hmmm. It looks like seven of those miles are going either up or down at a rate close to 1,000 feet per mile. The rest of it looks to be fairly easy, except the terrain between Toothache Ridge and Blister Butte is rocky, and it has been raining lately.

Hmmm. This isn't exactly a tote road in the jackpine flats of the Huron National Forest. Let's think about this one. In fact let's start to divide the whole world of backpacking up into easy, moderate, and severe terrain. That way we can remove the discussion from what I think is easy or what you think is easy.

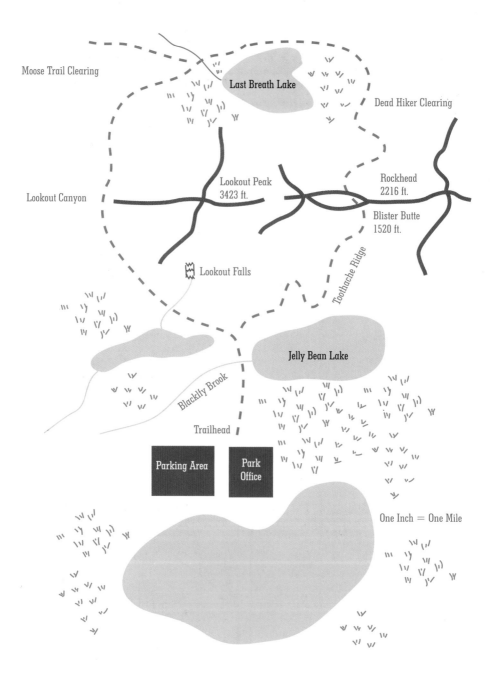

Moose Trail Clearing

Last Breath Lake

Dead Hiker Clearing

Lookout Peak
3423 ft.

Rockhead
2216 ft.

Lookout Canyon

Blister Butte
1520 ft.

Lookout Falls

Toothache Ridge

Jelly Bean Lake

Blackfly Brook

Trailhead

Parking Area

Park
Office

One Inch = One Mile

FIGURE 2

*A typical trail map for a fictitious trail that can be aquired at the trailhead
office. Always consider terrain and elevation; it looks like a short 11-mile walk,
but the terrain and elevation make it more difficult.*

Easy Terrain. Easy terrain is flat, or nearly so, and the footing is secure. A bog is flat—but there's no way you can relax and let out your stride. Soft sand may be better—but not much. Forest roads, trails following streams that don't come downhill at a severe rate, rolling hills—these are generally easy walking, and you can plan for 2 miles an hour, including breaks. Sure, you could go faster, but why bother? If you want to race, take up race walking, where everybody is competing and knows it. Don't inflict a sneaky sort of competition on your companions when they know neither the game nor the rules.

Moderate Terrain. I have a tendency to call easy terrain "moderate" when I'm dealing with novices, unless they're gorillas, because if you haven't backpacked, no terrain is really easy. However, to quantify "moderate" I'd call it a trail that's mostly solid underfoot, with either one pretty stiff hill in it somewhere or a series of little ones.

You can charge along and still make 2 miles an hour, but best figure 1.5 miles per hour. This lets you stop to smell the roses.

Which brings up another point. Even if you're tired, you're better off if you walk steadily and fall into a mindless rhythm, stopping for long enough to refresh yourself, rather than if you drag along and never stop. Smell the roses, by all means. But take the time to smell them thoroughly, and then let yourself become absorbed in the simple and joyful act of walking.

Severe Terrain. Any terrain in which you ascend or descend over 500 feet in a mile of trail is severe. And don't let any Trail Animal convince you otherwise. When you know the game better, you'll question this statement, too. But don't question it now, don't question it ever in public, and don't question it ever when you talk to people backpacking as a family.

The fact is that most trails in mountainous country ascend and descend at about 1000 feet per mile, which is like climbing a long, gentle staircase, except it will vary from flat or nearly so to places where there may literally be ladders to scale. Western trails, which have frequently been designed to accommodate horses, are generally less steep but take a lot longer to get where they're going. Is 10 miles of 500-feet-per-mile ascent worse than 5 miles of 1,000-feet-per-mile ascent? I can't tell you. I know I'd rather descend the longer, gentler slope. Steep descents are as debilitating to your leg muscles as steep ascents, particularly when you're carrying your house on your back.

In severe terrain plan on a mile an hour. You'll still have time to smell the roses—but you'll be huffin' and puffin' when you do.

With these measurements in mind, we see now that the jaunt back into Dead Hiker Clearing is no piece of cake. Seven of those miles are taken at 1 mile per hour and three are taken at 1.5 miles per hour; that's nine hours so far, and we still have that 0.73 mile to take care of. Okay, it's a piece of cake, but it's the last of the trail, and it takes an hour. That's ten hours of walking. That's too much right now. It may be too much anytime, unless it's a flat-out emergency.

Were the folks back at your outfitter's deliberately misleading you when they called it an easy jaunt? Maybe. There are some people—all of whom swear that they're not competitive—who'll brag about something like this. It's like the paddlers who call a solid Class IV drop a Class II, so when you eat it, they can posture and look like heroes.

More than likely, though, you dropped in on weekend warriors swapping stories with the shop people. These are hard people. They carry a minimum of very high quality, lightweight gear, and they're in superb condition for backpacking. You'd find, if you asked them, that they're active year-round. They ski, they paddle, they ride bicycles. They make the effort to learn techniques for biomechanical activities. They like to do things well. They probably blaze into Dead Hiker Clearing in five hours, smell all the roses on the way twice, stop for lunch and maybe even a snooze, and get to the clearing in time to scramble up the cirque wall on Blister Butte. They're for real.

And you know something? If you went backpacking with them, they'd travel at a pace comfortable for you. Remember that when you become a Certified Trail Animal. As the old-time horse players used to say, "Class shows when there is no class."

CHAPTER 2

Basic Gear for Walking in the Woods

Check this chapter heading again, please. We're talking about walking in the woods. We're not talking about hero treks along the crest of the Continental Divide. When it's time to do that, you'll be writing your own book. But right now, we want to look over some gear that'll make your walk in the woods a pleasure—and that you won't *outgrow*.

Let's consider this a moment. When I talk about gear you won't outgrow, I'm not talking about size. I'm talking about quality. The old axiom that you buy cheap gear three or four times is never so true as it is with outdoor gear. Get a cheap pack if you wish; just be prepared for it to never work well, to never be comfortable, and to require replacement after only limited use. This isn't an argument for buying the top-of-the-line gear, with bells and whistles. The time may come when the bells and whistles are useful to you; for now, it's doubtful that you need a loop for your ice axe and straps for carrying crampons. What you're shopping for should fit well, look good, and hold up in use.

What you're shopping for specifically are a few items that will make your life easier in the outback, and something in which to carry them. That "something" is commonly called a daybag, a day pack, or a small backpack. And we're not going to talk about the pack first. Why not? Because until you have a pretty good idea of what's going into the pack, the size and shape of the pack itself are absolutely meaningless.

You could probably make up a list of what you need for a day's walk in the woods in spring, summer, or fall without my help if you thought about it for a minute, but I'll help you enjoy.

Water. This is the one indispensable item in any wilderness traveler's kit, for reasons that are both obvious and far too extensive to go into here. You can't depend on finding drinkable water anywhere close to human habitation and only rarely out in the boondocks. You either go prepared to treat water to make it drinkable, or you carry water with you.

For a short scoot in the woods, the simple approach is to carry water with you. So you'll need something in which to carry it. Rummage through your outfitter's shelves until you find a wide-mouthed plastic bottle that will hold about a liter. I prefer water bottles made of Lexan, because Lexan doesn't pick up flavors as readily as some other plastics (see Figure 3). Why a wide-mouthed bottle rather than a narrow-mouthed canteen? Simple. It's easier to fill, and it's easier to mix stuff like lemonade in a wide-mouthed bottle. Get one for every family member who's walking with you.

If you'd rather get water as you go, plan on carrying some form of

FIGURE 3

Wide-mouthed Lexan water bottles are more suitable for backpacking than small-mouthed canteens. (Photo: Nalgene)

treatment. Iodine tablets or crystals are the lightest and least expensive option. If you want to be fancy and carry a water filter, be prepared to spend some money. Boiling water is also an effective treatment, but that takes considerable time and you're probably not going to carry a stove on a day hike. Either way, carry something to treat water. If not, you're gambling, and the stakes are high.

Food. If you aren't troubled with metabolic problems like diabetes or hypoglycemia, going a day without food will not hurt you a bit. However, this isn't the time to either go on a diet or start the practice of fasting.

It isn't the time to go on a sugar binge, either. The mild exercise you get from walking will trigger a low-level release of stored glycogens from your liver after you've gone through the sugars in your bloodstream, so you don't need five pounds of chocolate bars.

Here's what I take: cheese and crackers, raisins or dried apricots, an energy bar, and something sweet that won't melt. There is chocolate that won't melt: It's called M&M's. Mix these gaudy little dudes with some dry roasted peanuts in a ziplock bag, and you'll be "good to go," as my old point guard was fond of saying.

Do yourself a favor. Repackage your snacks in ziplock bags. Put a hunk of cheese in one, and toss crackers, a few handfuls of dried fruit, and chocolate all in their own bags. This way you can reseal what you don't eat, you don't end up carrying more than you'll eat, and the food stays fresh and sealed so you won't come home with a pack full of cracker crumbs.

Your favorite outdoor outfitter will have an assortment of freeze-dried and dehydrated food packets you might consider preparing. Sometimes the meals are extravagant, but for the most part they are very easy to prepare. Again, it is important to consult a helpful salesperson to get a little experienced advice.

The benefit in taking along freeze-dried and dehydrated fare is the weight of these products as opposed to that of groceries. With the water extracted from the food, the weight load is reduced by more than 50 percent. This is most important when cross-country trekking; however, you might wish to make it easy on your back on shorter trips, also.

First-Aid Kit. State-of-the-art dressings, wound-closure tapes, and nonprescription medications allow the construction of a very useful first-aid kit for general outdoor use.

Very often treatments can be improvised with items on hand, but prior planning and the inclusion of key items in your kit will provide you with the best that modern medical science can offer.

Most outfitting stores carry prepackaged first-aid kits. Outdoor Research, REI, and Adventure Medical offer good ones. You can also make your own. Here's what I take:

- Non-latex surgical gloves, several pairs
- Cover-strip closures (2 packages)
- Moleskin
- Spenco Second Skin
- Bulb irrigating syringe
- Gauze pads (5 packages)
- Gauze dressing (2 rolls)
- Elastic bandage (roll, Ace Bandage)
- Tape, hypoallergenic
- Hydrocortisone cream
- Triple antibiotic ointment
- Antimicrobial skin cleanser
- Medications (laxative, antidiarrhea, allergy, decongestant, antihistamine, aspirin, ibuprofen, etc.)
- Sterile swabs
- Safety pins
- Extra vials and resealable plastic bags for repackaging the above
- Black Sharpie marker and paper
- Reference cards or packable first-aid guide
- Extra supply of any special medications necessary to treat known conditions of members of your party

Of course, the kit is only part of it; you must know how to use the contents of the kit. Brush up on your skills with a general first-aid course at your local Red Cross or YMCA. If you're interested in learning about more advanced medical techniques, there are a number of terrific courses that deal specifically with first aid in the backcountry. For more information, contact SOLO (Stonehearth Open Learning Opportunities), the Wilderness Medicine Institute, the Wilderness Medical Associates, or the National Association for Search and Rescue.

Raingear. Chances are that it rains where you live. Chances are that it will rain on you sometime when you're moseying through the forest. Most rational beings won't set out for a walk in the woods when the fall gales hit the upper Great Lakes or the rains hit the Georgia coastal plains; but if you wait for that perfect day when there is no threat of rain at all, you won't do much walking. You're not made of sugar; you won't melt.

But you'll think you're made of sugar if your raingear doesn't work well. Now, "work well" is one of those wonderful weasel phrases beloved of outdoor writers who either choose not to go into detail or don't spend enough time outside to know what's happening. What works well today for me may not work well for you today, even if you're walking beside me.

Why? A lot of reasons. I may be expending a bit less energy and perspiring less. I may be more comfortable on a hot, humid day, and because I'm fussing less, I'm less prone to being bothered by a little condensation. I may be walking with a thin polypropylene undershirt under my rain jacket, and you may have a heavy cotton/poly blend T-shirt on, which traps moisture and makes you feel damp. I may have

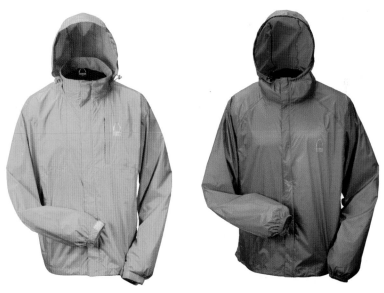

FIGURE 4

A hooded rain jacket with detachable hood (left) and an open-collar rain jacket (right). (Photos: Sierra Designs)

Raingear comparison

	ADVANTANGES	DISADVANTAGES
Gore-Tex	Waterproof; breathable; excellent construction; perfect for cool and coldweather	Expensive; impractical for warm-weather walking
Activent/DWR	Mostly waterproof; breathable; less expensive than Gore-Tex	More expensive than a poncho; not completely waterproof
Plastic	Very inexpensive	Traps perspiration; not breathable; practically disposable

taken the time to ventilate trapped warm air from inside the jacket by loosening my collar, and I may have chosen to wear a hat rather than pull up the hood on my jacket, which effectively insulated the nape of my neck and my throat—two areas that are critical in heat regulation. In simpler terms, it's a combination of good raingear and good sense that keeps you comfortable. Good raingear alone makes the job easier, but it's no guarantee of comfort.

Raingear can be divided into two designs: the poncho and the commonly used rain jacket/rain pants sets. The poncho is big, a pain in the neck in a breeze, relatively easy to ventilate, and if you're looking for double-duty from your gear, downright hazardous in a canoe or on a bicycle. Rain jackets (see Figure 4) and rain pants are more versatile, require more care in use to maintain adequate ventilation, are more comfortable in a wind, and can, indeed, serve as wind garments. If I was limiting my outings to generally warm weather and didn't want to spend a lot of money on raingear, I'd opt for a poncho. If I wanted more versatility, I'd get lightweight, coated nylon rain pants and a rain jacket. I'd make sure the hood was comfortable; I'd try to keep pockets to a minimum; I'd like to see armpit zippers for extra ventilation; I'd prefer that the jacket didn't have elastic in the wrists, because elasticized wrists are difficult to ventilate; I'd prefer a drawcord waist and a fly front on the pants (ventilation again), and I'd like short zippers at the ankles so I could pull the pants on and off without taking my boots off. Would I look at one of the waterproof/breathable fabrics like Gore-Tex? Probably not, unless I was planning to do a lot of cool- and cold-weather walking for long periods of time. Would I look at one of the mostly water-proof jackets that are made of something like Activent or DWR (durable water-repellent finish)? Probably. You can't beat their versatility.

Warmwear. For most woods walking, you can scrounge through your dresser and your closet. The summer foray rarely requires more than a light sweater held in reserve and a pair of loose, comfortable shorts or pants. Please note that "loose and comfortable" does not include jeans or cut-off jeans, which are usually cut wrong for walking and soak up water like a sponge.

If you like things that are techy—and that just plain work—pick up a lightweight polypropylene underwear top and a lightweight fleece jacket or pullover. The combination of undershirt and fleece is cozy in even quite cool weather, yet breathable enough to be a pleasant addi-tion in the morning or at twilight on even a warm day. *Hint:* The polypro undershirt should have long sleeves; it's a bit of sun protection with essentially zero warmth when worn by itself. How did I find that out? On a two-week canoe trip (with a lot of ground exploration) in the Florida Everglades. Winter underwear in the subtropics!

For warm and cold walking, there is one rule to live by: Cotton kills. Even on a warm day, it is not difficult to catch a chill once you sit down for a while and feel a light breeze blow through your drenched cotton shirt. Cotton absorbs moisture and takes a long time to dry. It also sticks to your skin and prevents a layer of air from forming between your clothes and your body. It is this layer of air that keeps you warm; without it, you get chilled. You can suffer from hypothermia when it's as warm as 50 degrees Fahrenheit, so use your common sense and leave the cotton at home.

Compass. You'll want one, even if you might not need it right away. Besides, a compass is even more fun than a good diamond whetstone as a time-waster. And who knows? You never can tell when you'll need a sharp

FIGURE 5

Your personal backpacking gear might include binoculars, a guidebook, a flashlight, and a pocket knife.

knife or the esoteric map-and-compass skills you honed during lunch.

Get a compass with a transparent base plate, the kind you can lay on a map and use for real navigation. Forget the little round jobs with wiggly (induction-damped) needles, as they're less accurate and a pain to use. Ten bucks or so will get you a very reliable instrument that's capable of greater accuracy than you can use.

Personal Gear. This is another one of those wonderful catchall phrases that can cover everything from a camera to a few sheets of toilet paper. For a day's walk in the woods, take what you will need and what will enrich the jaunt. When you're carrying your whole house on your back, you have to be more ruthless with your whims, or you'll wind up toting 40 pounds of lightweight, high-tech stuff you don't need.

What do I think is necessary for a random scoot in my nearby Huron National Forest? Sunglasses, lip balm with 15 SPF, sunscreen, insect repellent (which I very rarely use), a pocket knife, binoculars (mine are big old fat ones), a bird guide and wildflower guide, and a small notebook and pen (see Figure 5). To me, a walk in the woods is a time for both external and internal exploration. You may be happier with a Frisbee and a harmonica. But don't forget the bug dope, sunscreen, sunglasses, and lip balm!

Where to Put All This. In a pack, of course. But not the pack you'll be using for overnighting and longer trips. For day trips you want a small pack that will comfortably hold everything you'll need, with a little extra capacity for winter jaunts (see Figure 6).

FIGURE 6

A daypack.
(Photo: Kelty)

My wife and I each have a small day pack and midsize backpack from which to choose, and the most common pairing is one small pack each. In cooler weather one of us will take the larger backpack. In winter we'll take a large backpack if we plan to have something hot for lunch.

When you go looking for small and midsize packs, you'll face a bewildering variety of gear and wide price range. Keep these hints in mind as you look:

1. Bells and whistles are only useful if they're bells you usually ring and whistles you usually blow.

2. While a subframe is usually superfluous for a light pack, a thin foam pad built into the pack helps the pack keep its shape, helps it to carry better, and keeps the edges of your bird guide from excavating a hole in your back. It is not sissy to be comfortable. Just remember old Nessmuk's classic dictum from the turn of the last century: "We do not go into the woods to rough it. We go to smooth it. We get it rough enough in town."

3. Even the most slender waistband helps to keep the pack stabilized and keeps it from bouncing. You don't need to worry about magical phrases like "transferring the weight to your hips" when you're carrying eight pounds.

4. Firmly padded shoulder straps are mandatory.

5. Lots of cute little pockets and zippers look official but are usually more trouble than they're worth. However, a pack that's divided

FIGURE 7

Getting packs for your kids is a good investment.

into top and bottom compartments is well worth the price, and a larger backpack with either a header (the pocket on the flap), a front pocket, or side pockets (make sure they fit your water bottle or buy water bottles to fit) is very handy to use.

6. The price of a pack reflects its materials and its sewing time (for which read "complexity"). By and large, you get what you pay for.

7. If you hike with kids, remember that they'll fuss if they carry a tiny pack, and they'll fuss more if they don't. Make them a part of an adventure rather than an onerous duty. If you walk with kids, get packs for the kids (Figure 7).

Strangely enough, probably the second most important piece of backpacking gear (after your head) is neither bedroom nor kitchen nor pack. It's what you wear on your feet, which is more than just a pair of boots. And if we didn't talk about boots when we were chatting about a day's walk in the woods, it's because casual walking with next to no equipment on your back can be done in casual footgear. Specialized terrain requires at least a look at more specialized shoes, and putting

20 to 25 percent of your weight on your back and schlepping it up hill and down dale requires more than a look, unless you're young, strong, immune to pain, and plan to live forever. So let's look at boots (and how to walk in them!)

Boots. The word "boots" has a solid, honest ring to it. There are shoes, made to look pretty and to protect my feet from dog droppings and broken glass. And there are boots, made to keep my feet comfortable and provide a solid working platform while I roam around in that wonderful country north of Highway 20. There's a difference.

Time was when boots were made of full-hide roughout or smoothout leather. Period. They weighed maybe 5 pounds per pair, took forever to break in, required maintenance, and were nearly indestructible. That was then. In 1968 these high-quality boots could be had for under sixty dollars a pair. Today? Don't ask.

But this might not be something to fret about. I think we made too much of a fetish of the Superboot back then. Lightweight boots didn't provide an adequate sense of heroism. Real Men, by God, wore Real Boots!

I still have a pair of Real Boots, bench-made by the French firm of Galibier. They're masterpieces. And unless I was going on a snow or mixed-snow-and-ice climb where I needed crampons, you wouldn't ever find me wearing them. They're just too much boot.

The modern criteria for backpacking footgear is "fit, fit, and fit." Yes, your footgear should be sufficiently sturdy to hold together

The right fit

- Choose a boot that is sturdy but lightweight.
- Try on boots in the socks you plan to wear on your walk.
- Walk around the store for a half hour to make sure the fit is comfortable.
- Can you wiggle your toes in the boot? If not, try a larger size.
- Is your heel snug? Yes? Good.
- Does the tongue of the boot rest comfortably along the top of your foot?
- Make sure the width of the boot matches the width of your foot.

FIGURE 8

A thick outer sock.

(Photo: SmartWool)

throughout a trip. Yes, it should provide protection for your feet. Yes, it should provide a firm foundation for walking and scrambling. But it need not be bombproof, it need not last forever, and it need not be waterproof.

Good grief! Harry Roberts, the Last of the Old-Time Tech Warriors, advocating what amounts to "throw-away" boots?

Yeah. Sort of. We have seen a genuine revolution in backcountry footgear. Today's boots are derived from athletic shoe technology and are essentially untouched by human hands in manufacture. They are light, comfortable right out of the box, engineered by some person who has made computer studies of what happens to feet when their owner is toting a pack up a hill, and functional. Do they last forever? Who cares?

Let me expand on that idea a bit. The only activities I can think of where the durability of a piece of equipment is often considered to be more important than the functionality of the equipment are backpacking and canoeing. I'm constantly mystified at this. I'm even more mystified at the collateral notion that "performance" is a dirty word, right up there with "stylish" in the lexicon of the average outdoorsperson. Thank you, I'll carry the very light tent, even if it requires more care and even if it won't withstand a summit gale on Mt. Rainier. Thank you, I'll paddle the quick canoe that weighs under 50 pounds, even if it might be a hair less rugged than a plastic bruisewater. Thank you, I'll ski on the very lightest touring skis that meet my needs rather than on some flattened water rollers that will withstand collision with a tree. Why? Because the gear that's light, responsive, and designed to perform is simply a lot more fun to use. It may take a little more skill—or even a lot more skill—to learn to pitch the tent in a sheltered area, or miss the rocks with the canoe (yes, you can miss the rocks!), or miss the tree on your skis. But you spend your life doing skill-oriented things—unless you regularly stop your automobile by bumping it off the end of your garage!

Get the neat stuff, the light stuff, the fun stuff, and learn to use it. That way, you'll return again and again to the out-back, and you'll enjoy it more each time. Get the clunky stuff, and you won't enjoy it—unless you're into self-flagellation.

FIGURE 9
A gaiter.
(Photo: Outdoor Research)

You will want to choose a boot from the lightweight or midweight category. There is a broad range of prices and styles, so ask your local outfitter to help you find the boot that's right for you.

Footgear as a Total Concept. The boot is only part of the equation. Generally when you buy a pair of boots—or shoes of any sort—you try them on with the type of socks you plan to wear with them. Otherwise, the shoe won't fit the same on the trail as it did in the store. The socks, then, are a critical part of the whole protection package for your feet. In years past, hikers would often wear two pairs of socks one thick, heavy wool sock and one lighter liner. The reasoning behind this was two-fold: itch and blister prevention.

Well, times have certainly changed. With a well-fitting, properly laced boot today's hiker needs only one pair of high-quality hiking socks. And, while the technology behind the sock has changed, the fabric has not. Today's technical hiking sock is still constructed from wool, but it's higher quality merino wool, the world's most efficient fab-ric. For example, SmartWool has designed a performance hiking sock that uses a SmartFit system for an all day, athletic fit. The socks absorb perspiration in its vapor state and releases it before it condenses into moisture, so feet stay drier and bacteria doesn't build up. Result: more comfort, less odor, and NO blisters.

But footgear encompasses more than boots and socks. If the trend in contemporary bootmaking is toward lightweight boots, which may be somewhat less protective and waterproof than boots of the past, it behooves you to look for sneaky little ways to increase protection without greatly increasing weight. Let's look at a piece of gear that was very popular with both backpackers and ski tourers in the past—ironically, when boots were heavier. It's called the gaiter (see Figure 9). It's nothing more than a tube of coated nylon, with a zipper or Velcro up the side, and a cord that goes under the boot sole. It covers the top of your boot and excludes rain, ticks, sand, pebbles, and other things that make walking a chore. Gaiters—low-cut ones for three-season travel—are simply worth their weight in gold. Don't leave home without them.

CHAPTER 3

The House You Live In

The house you live in on the trail is a system made up of tent, tarp, ground cloth, sleeping pad, and sleeping bag. Before we get into a discussion about gear and its use, let me preface this whole bag of worms with one simple statement and one simple conclusion.

The statement is this: The house you live in is the heaviest part of your gear.

And the conclusion that inevitably follows: The less your house weighs, the easier it will be to carry.

The Tent. You'll need a small two-person tent—or larger if you plan to hike with the family. It may be a modified A-frame (with curved poles fore and aft in the form of an A and a single pole in the rear), or perhaps a dome tent, with plenty of head-room and living space (see Figure 10). Unless you're planning on camping on the Catenary Ridge of Mt. Logan or some equally insane spot, you're not interested in a tent's ability to stand up to 60-knot winds.

Let me digress about winds. I've lived in one of the few wooded spots in the country where wind-power generation is feasible and economically sound. The typical day is 10- to 20-knot winds. In autumn, what Gordon Lightfoot called "the gales of November," which may actually run from October through December, are a fact of life. I can remember one day

FIGURE 10

An A-frame tent (top) and a
dome tent, shown without a
rain fly (bottom).
(Photos: Johnson
Outdoors, Inc./
Eureka)

of winds in excess of 60 knots up on the shores of Lake Huron. Don't go blithely talking about 60-knot winds—or listening to people talking about them with absolute credulity—until you've experienced one. The chance of encountering one on a valley floor in wooded country is so remote as to be effectively out of the question.

In short, then, three things really dictate your choice: space, weight, and convenience. They're all interrelated, but we can look at them separately.

Space is largely self-explanatory. Just keep in mind that space considerations are three-dimensional. For example: My wife and I are long, stringy people who can coexist in a narrow tent quite well. However, we need more headroom than would a shorter couple, and we'll sacrifice tent width for tent height and tent length, unless the extra height and length add too much weight.

Space is also a function of ventilation. A small tent with large screens and a good flow of air is felt to be more roomy than a larger tent with small vent space. Also, a dark tent is perceived as smaller. Some people like to feel that the tent is small. It becomes, for them, a safe, snug, dry cave. Others need room. How do you find out what you prefer? Go to your local outfitter and climb into the tents that interest you. And if you hike with your spouse, bring your spouse. Both of you have to agree on the desirability of the tent.

Weight is so important that it must be considered with every piece of gear. We've already established that the tent needn't be bombproof, because you're not camping on exposed ridges, and you're an adult who takes care of your toys. Indestructibility is way down your priority list.

The equation is simple. The larger the tent, the more fabric it takes to make it, and the more pole sections it takes to support it. You can, with some tents, choose aluminum or carbon fiber poles and save a pound or more. Bring money. It's a worthwhile trade. "Well, it weighs 5 pounds more, but it saved me eighty dollars," is small consolation halfway up Blister Butte in a rainstorm.

What's an acceptable weight for a two-person tent that will turn weather away and be more than a portable doghouse? I'd like to think about 5 pounds total, including tent, fly, pole set, stakes, and stuff bag.

Convenience is something only you can determine. And you can determine it only by setting the tent up a few times at your outfitter's store. If something deep down inside tells you that you'll never adapt to that nifty storm closure at three in the morning when the rain starts and you're still foggy from sleep, don't get the tent. If it takes forever to set up, or needs four different pole sets, all of which differ by an inch in length and you can't tell one from the other until they're all in place, don't get the tent. I don't care how neat looking it is—if you wouldn't want to set it up in a hard rain, don't get the tent.

Erecting Your House. Remember what all the books on camping and backpacking told you about where to pitch your tent? Here's a

Choosing a tent—what to look for

- Most modern tents usually have a large vestibule (see Figure 11) or extension of the rain fly that can be used for cooking in a downpour and to store muddy boots and wet dogs. Look for a spacious and sturdy vestibule.
- Aluminum or carbon fiber poles are the lightest.
- Are there enough mesh doors and windows for adequate ventilation?
- Avoid single-wall tents.
- Is the tent large enough for you, the people you hope to take with you, and your gear to comfortably spend the night?
- Are there inner pockets to hold your flashlight or contact lenses?
- How much does it weigh? Can you carry it all day on your back?

sample, in case you missed all that schlog—or in case you need a belly laugh to get through the day.

"Seek out a spot that's high and dry, grassy but not boggy, facing the east so the morning sun will cheer you, and shaded, but not under trees that might blow over on you in a storm, or draw lightning to you. Further, the site should be close to potable water and should have copious firewood nearby."

There may be ten such spots in the continental United States that aren't for sale for $2,743 a square foot. There are maybe forty such in Canada—but that's the good news. The bad news is that you have to walk 186 miles to get to all of them, and most of them require the ascent and descent of 12,000-foot ice walls.

Where, in these days of crowded trails and densely packed designated camping areas in the backcountry, do you make your home? *Anywhere you can find a flat spot.*

This is the problem. We've exceeded the carrying power of the range, as it were. We all want the magical experience; we all head to the legendary places to walk, just as we all head to the legendary places to paddle and to ski. And these places are neat. That's why they became legends in the first place. But keep in mind that the legendary places usually had the benefit of either good press-agentry or were proximate to a major metropolitan area, or both. This certainly helped both the White Mountains and the Adirondacks, and some of the prime western areas have been puffed up by the media as well. Meanwhile I can start from my front door and walk across the upper part of Michigan's Lower Peninsula on a wonderful trail that courses through the jackpine, sand, and bog ecology of the Huron and Manistee National Forests and have the place to myself. That's where two of those ten campsites are, in fact!

Don't get me wrong. A walk through the jackpines in Michigan is not the same experience as a walk through Indian Henry's Hunting Ground on the Wonderland Trail, with Mt. Rainier looming over your shoulder to the northeast and the valley of Tahoma Creek and Emerald Ridge in your face. In fact I'm not sure that anywhere on earth comes up to the Wonderland as a constantly varied scenic experience. But spectacular scenery isn't the only reason we walk. There are no sweeping vistas on the Shore-to-Shore Trail in Michigan. But the bird life is profuse and varied, the biota varies with 20 feet of elevation gain and loss, and while it's mostly jackpine, you begin to gain an appreciation for good old *Pinus banksiana* as a forest tree. It may be a junk tree in some places, but up here, halfway between the equator and the north pole, it's what grows, and you learn to love it. There are quiet places in the world where you learn to look in deep rather than out far. My Michigan is one of them. So are the Georgia coast and the Everglades.

So, in all probability, is the country around where you live. Get to know it, and you most likely can find a level, breezy, dry campsite that's close to potable water—or close to water, at any rate. Don't pass up a trip to the great places, ever. But don't ever define them as the only places where backpacking exists. Because it exists everywhere. And it's good everywhere.

Okay. So we might not find the perfect place to pitch a tent. What can we do about it?

A fair amount, actually, particularly if you keep in mind that the tent is simply shelter for the night, not a permanent abode. If you're setting up the tent as a base camp for day hikes, you may want to scrounge for a quality site, because you may want to spend a day hanging out at

FIGURE 11

A tent with a vestibule. Vestibules make storing gear and cooking in the rain a cinch! (Photo: Johnson Outdoors, Inc./Eureka)

base camp, reading and renewing yourself. On the other hand, you could always move you and your book and your sleeping pad a quarter-mile to a neat flat rock in the sun with little effort.

Try for the ideal site, obviously. Of all the criteria, I'd choose "smooth and level" above all if it didn't look like rain, and "high and dry" if it did. However, there isn't much I can do about "smooth and level" if the site isn't that way to begin with, assuming that I'm smart enough to remove loose stones and sticks, but there is something I can do about keeping relatively dry in a relatively wet campsite.

Several things, in fact.

First, make sure you've sealed all the seams exposed to rain, wind-blown rain, and groundwater in both the tent and the fly sheet. This isn't an onerous job. Pick a rain-free day, set up the tent, and do it. Take your time. Fuss over it. Enjoy the rapport with Old Buddy Tent.

In all honesty, seam-sealing isn't 100 percent effective. But it helps; it gives you an edge, as it were, and it is certainly something that's within your power to control.

That you do at home. This you do at home and in the field: If it looks like a rainy weekend, or if you're going out for a longer trip, or if you're the belt-and-suspenders type, tote with you either a piece of 4mm plastic (found in any hardware store) that's a few inches larger in all dimensions than your tent floor, or tote a piece of coated nylon taffeta—the lightweight stuff, 2 ounces per yard nominal—of similar dimensions, and use that as a ground cloth. But a ground cloth with a difference. *This* ground cloth doesn't go on the ground. It goes *inside* the tent. Why? Because water can't sneak between the tent floor and the ground cloth when the ground cloth is inside. It can otherwise, and it will be driven through the tent floor and into your bedroom. Ground cloth inside, then. Just like a rug.

The third thing is all field work. If it looks like rain, make sure your rain fly is properly secured over the tent. Stake the rain fly so the material is taut. Pull the material as tight as it will go and cinch the straps as far as they'll go. Make it so tight that the raindrops actually "ping" when they bounce off it and the water runs right off the fly and doesn't get trapped in a crease or pool up on top of the tent. If the water gets caught, it will cause the material to sag. If the rain fly sags into the tent, water will seep right through, and then you'll have a problem.

And that's about all you need to know about setting up tents. If you have a new tent, it helps to practice setting it up once or twice before you have to set it up in the dark, and it helps old hands to unpack their Old Buddy Tent before they leave, set it up, and check for things that may have been lost or misplaced from the last trip. Yes, I have left my little stake bag at home! That's not a total loss; stakes can be readily fashioned. But the fancy aluminum pole sets for a dome tent can't be. Leave those at home and you have a problem!

Sleeping Bags and Pads. In the past this would have been the time for a learned disquisition on the internal structure of down sleeping bags and a solemn, sententious treatise on the differences between down and synthetic insulation.

I don't think we need to go through that again. The choices are simple. So are the tradeoffs. Down is lighter per unit thickness. It is more compressible, which means it fits into a smaller stuff bag than a synthetic bag of the same size and thickness. It is more sensitive to

Down vs. synthetic sleeping bags

DOWN	SYNTHETIC
Generally warmer than a synthetic bag of a comparable degree rating	Generally sleeps a little cooler
More compact	Slightly more bulky
Weighs less	Weighs a little more
Dries more slowly	Dries more quickly

atmospheric moisture and perspiration than synthetic fill, but you can completely discard the old notion that "you can't sleep in a wet down bag, but you can in a wet synthetic bag." You can't sleep in either one! However, you can dry the synthetic bag in the field. But how in the world did you get your sleeping bag that wet anyway?

Consider this: If your sleeping bag is stuffed in its little nylon house called a stuff bag and is inside your pack, it's tough to get it wet. In fact, take a down bag well stuffed and try to get it wet by immersing it in a sink filled with water. You'll wet a little at the mouth of the stuff sack, and that's all. This means that if you've gotten your sleeping bag truly, thoroughly wet, you probably managed to do that by leaving it on a flat rock to air out and left it there during a hard rain. At that point, sleep in your pile jacket, lightweight long johns, and stocking cap with your feet stuffed into your pack, and consider that a benign deity chose to merely inconvenience you for your oversight rather than kill you.

Given a choice of bags, I'd choose a mummy (see Figure 12) in the 20- to 30-degree range and, what with the development of highly compressible synthetic insulations, it might well be a synthetic bag. Knowing my taste for neat stuff, though, and my general desire to go light, I might choose a down-filled mummy in the same comfort range.

Now, "comfort range" is another weasel phrase. There are times when I'm comfortable at 10 degrees in a "30-degree" bag, and there are times when nothing short of a waterbed with the temperature cranked up to "womb" will do.

You see, sleeping comfortably depends on skill, in the long run.

It depends on how well you manage your caloric intake and your fluid intake, for one. Try to walk off some body fat in the outback, and you'll probably be chilly. Go without fluid on a cool day when you don't feel thirsty and walk off 3 percent of your body weight (that's only 4.5 pounds for a 150-pounder), and you'll be chilly. Walk off 5 percent of your body weight and you might become a medical emergency in a big hurry.

Hang around the campfire in damp, sweaty clothing and you'll sleep cold. Wear damp clothing in your sleeping bag and you'll sleep cold. Put your sleeping bag on the ground—tent floor and ground cloth don't count for warmth—and you'll sleep cold. Wind down the day with three good jolts of 100 proof "to warm you up" and you'll sleep cold. Smoke and you'll sleep cold.

And chances are you'll blame the sleeping bag!

How to sleep warm? Use a foam sleeping pad or a lightweight air-filled mattress that can be inflated for extra comfort. (Mine is called a Therm-A-Rest, and it's as much a part of my overnighting gear as my head.) That buys you quite a few degrees of comfort. Eat regularly and lightly; don't stuff yourself and hit the sack. Maintain a proper fluid balance. Drink water—and don't mix it half and half with Mr. Jack. Wear dry underclothing (or nothing at all) in your sleeping bag. If you wake up chilly, a mouthful of water sometimes helps. So might a mouthful of trail mix—but don't keep that in the tent, please. A bear next to you would keep you plenty warm, but not in a way you'd really like. And wear a hat. I take a funky old red woolen watch cap with me even on canoeing trips in Florida. This hat has been

FIGURE 12

A mummy-style sleeping bag.
(Photo: Johnson Outdoors, Inc./Eureka)

Three types of sleeping pads

	ADVANTAGES	DISADVANTAGES
Closed-cell foam	Basic, lightweight, inexpensive, indestructible	Not very comfortable
Open-cell foam	Very light, compacts easily	Absorbs water
Self-inflating	Most comfortable by far, compacts easily	Weighs more, not as durable as closed-cell foam

with me on some winter climbs in rough situations and on casual overnights with my kids on the "back mountain." Mostly it stays in my pack. But when I'm tired and it's chilly, it goes on, probably as early as when we make camp. The key to staying warm is to stay warm; don't get chilled in the first place. It's a lot harder to regain warmth than to *retain* warmth.

So, don't keep your shirt on. Keep your hat on.

CHAPTER 4

The Kitchen

We haven't talked much about food and the means of preparing it. It isn't easy to talk about food, except in generalizations, because some folks will build four-course meals over an open fire and whip up blueberry muffins for breakfast, while others would just as soon brew up that grim concoction known as freeze-dried veggie beef stew and wolf it down with neither joy nor enlightenment. I prefer to scrounge leftovers myself, bring nothing but Christian Brothers brandy and good coffee, and trade that for food. However, that doesn't always work, so I subsist nicely in that gray area between Campfire Cordon Bleu and Gutbomb Veggie Beef Stew.

I do have a few rules that I mostly follow:

Rule One is the Lazy Person's Rule. Never cook anything that takes more than one pot, unless it's a layover day and somebody else brought the extra pot.

Rule Two is the Hungry Person's Rule. Never cook anything that takes much more than fifteen minutes from pack to stomach.

Rule Three is the Contemplative Person's Rule. Before you unpack, before you even make camp, brew up a cup of soup or a cup of coffee, sprawl out on your Therm-A-Rest, and enjoy, enjoy. The only time to violate this rule is when it's raining, in which case you set up your tarp and then brew up the cup of comfort. Under those conditions, it's acceptable to opt for coffee and brandy, provided you share it.

Rule Four is the Thoughtful Person's Rule. Cooking is done over a camp stove. Campfire cooking is for absolute emergencies or for areas where there's so much dead and down wood that you might just as well use it. The catch there is that such areas are prime fire hazards. Play it wrong and you could burn down half of Saskatchewan.

Fortunately, the decision is usually taken from you. Many popular hiking areas prohibit fires, period. And in many others, the dead and down wood has been scrounged for a square mile around by three generations of romantics.

Don't misunderstand me. I like a small campfire, and where it's ecologically sane to build one, I will. There's something primordial about a campfire. You almost can see the eyes gleaming in the night at the edge of the fire's glow, and somewhere just beyond your hearing is the throaty rumble of a big cat. A romantic notion, perhaps. But I don't think many of us are immune to that kind of romance. I'm not, for sure.

Camp Stoves. But campfires are not cooking fires. Food is cooked over a camp stove (Figure 13), a one-burner job that may be fueled by white gas (more accurately, Coleman fuel), kerosene (rarely), butane or propane (very convenient but not very "hot"), alcohol, or a combination (multifuel stove). I use a butane stove a lot in summer. I recognize its

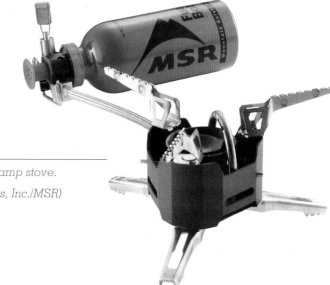

FIGURE 13

A modern lightweight camp stove.

(Photo: Cascade Designs, Inc./MSR)

limitations. It's bulky; the fuel cartridge can't be removed until all the fuel is used, so you can't change out just before a trip even though you know that the cartridge on the stove won't last; it's less than efficient in a wind; and you have "empties" to schlep back out. On the plus side, the little stove throttles down beautifully, lights instantly, and the cartridges can be changed out faster than filling a liquid fuel stove. I don't have the potential fire hazard of volatile liquid around, and I don't have to worry about the possibility of fuel leaking into the pack.

Use whatever best suits your temperament. There are times when I'm so relaxed that the quiet little butane stove, and its unhurried cooking pace, is just what I want. Other times I want to torch off my liquid fuel stove, boil the living hell out of something fast, and eat. I suspect you're the same. Neither of us wants to carry two stoves on a trip. So we settle for one, and we're wrong half the time. And it doesn't really matter. If I had to settle for one stove only, it would be a small pressurized liquid fuel stove like the MSR Dragonfly. And I would learn how to maintain it—and I'd maintain it before it needed maintenance. The time to diddle with a small stove is during the week, and the place is at home.

Food. Eat what you like, but don't spare the carbohydrates. That's what you run on.

Some hints: Most food—especially grocery store stuff—must be repackaged for easy storage. Also, there's no point in bringing a whole jar of instant coffee on an overnight when all you'll need is a few teaspoonfuls. If you don't need it, don't bring it. It's that simple.

However, I've always brought a few extras, specifically a few extra handfuls of pasta (macaroni, not spaghetti) and a couple packages of soup mix. Stuff the pasta and the soup mix in a heavy-duty ziplock bag, and forget it until you absolutely need it or you feel like a very bland change of pace.

There's a lesson here. If you divide the world up into belly fillers like rice, pasta, and instant mashed potatoes; protein sources like freeze-dried meats, beans, and nuts; sauces like soup mixes; gravy mixes; and veggies; you can sort of pick one from each column, throw them into the pot, and go for it. This isn't my system. It was created by June Fleming, who put it all into a book called *The Well-Fed Backpacker*, which was—and is—an absolute jewel of a no-nonsense how-to with a goodly touch of wit and the best thing ever on trail cooking. She calls this system "One-Liners," and she has six categories that can be combined into over 700,000 different meals, which should be

Some ideas for foods to get you started

Breakfasts	Lunches and Snacks	Dinners
Cereal	Jerky	Pasta with a variety of
Dehydrated milk	Soups	sauces
Toaster pastries	Peanut butter and	Dehydrated veggies
Oatmeal with raisins	crackers	Instant mashed
and brown sugar	Cheese and crackers	potatoes and gravy
Instant grits	Couscous	Beans
Instant cream of wheat	Tabouli	Soups
Instant coffee	Dried fruit	Quick-cook rice dishes
Tea bags	Nuts	Bread and butter
	Energy bars	
	Chocolate (nonmelting)	

Food tips Select foods that are:

Lightweight	Not going to spoil
Calorie-dense	Don't involve much packaging
Compact	Don't take more than fifteen minutes
	to prepare

more than enough to satisfy even the most jaded backpacker's appetite.

Here are some things I do that make cooking easier. Give them a try:

If I know I have to hydrate something recalcitrant for dinner, I put it into a wide-mouthed plastic jar with water and tote it in my pack for the day or for the afternoon. This can almost make the Dreaded Veggie Beef Stew palatable.

The backcountry is not the place to get casual about cleanup of cookware. If you're using only one pot for cooking—and very likely eating out of that pot—take the time to do a good, thorough cleanup of that pot. And not in the creek, please. What I do is torch off a teapotful of water while I'm eating. This gives me hot water for coffee and a reserve for pot washing. And it somehow makes the whole operation painless, if you know what I mean.

There is little use for a frypan on the trail, unless you plan to fish a lot. Otherwise, save the weight and leave it at home, unless it forms the cover of your cookset and you want it on to keep the nesting teapot, the cutlery, the potlifter, and the cleanup material from migrating. Of course, you can do all that with a stuff sack, which is lighter and keeps your pack clean. If you must take a frypan, get a coated one for easy cleanup, and get one with deep sides, so you can use it as a shallow pot.

If you use a liquid fuel stove, keep the stove and fuel bottle in an outside pocket of the pack. Don't stow them inside.

The Ultimate Simplicity Cookset for two people is one small stove, one 1½-quart pot, one nesting teapot (or 1-quart pot), two large cups, two tablespoons, one 1-quart wide-mouthed plastic bottle, a few small plastic vials containing some spices (oregano! Yeah!), and (if you can find one) a tiny ladle with a detachable handle. They come from France and they're wonderful. But that's for formal service. My wife and I simply eat out of the same pot most of the time.

Keep meals in proper perspective. Don't go hungry, but don't get bent out of shape if you're not serving gourmet food. You're not out there to cook.

Pray for the return of retort-pouch foods to the marketplace. Oh, how I looked forward to a toss-it-in-the-boiling-water treat of sweet and sour pork or shrimp Creole over a bed of rice cooked in the same pot at the same time! Great chow, that. Took about five minutes to prepare, and the taste was excellent. I know. Why carry water mixed with food when you have water out there? For convenience on a weekend is the answer. On a long trip, the extra weight would be distinctly burden-some. But for two days you can afford to live a little.

Remember, always, that you came out here to smell the flowers. While you're at it, enjoy the smell of your first cup of coffee in the morning.

CHAPTER 5

Container for Things Contained

Now, why in the world do we wait until nearly the end of a book on backpacking to talk about the backpack? I mean, isn't that the most important part of your gear?

Well . . . no. The most important part of your gear is what you carry in your head. One kilogram of wisdom and one gram of acceptance is worth tons of superlight, high-tech stuff.

Your pack is important, though. But it's neither more nor less important than any other piece of gear on which you depend, and it's considerably less important than the fit of your boots.

If you were to listen to some outfitters talk, or sit in on a Great Equipment Shootout at a camping area, you'd think that packs are right up there in complexity with things like F-15s, the human reproductive system, and great wine. C'mon, folks, let's be real. The human race has toted things on its collective back for millennia. There aren't that many secrets anymore!

But the few secrets are worth knowing.

And the first secret is the same one we talked about with boots. "Fit, fit, and fit" is the key to a comfortable pack. I wish I could give you some magic formula to ensure that your next pack—be it an internal-frame or an external-frame pack—will fit you perfectly. But I can't. Every pack out there might fit you just a bit differently and still work well. For example, I own two external-frame packs of rather different design. One is the

FIGURE 14

An external-frame pack.
(Photo: Kelty)

straightforward ladder frame with a padded hipbelt, and the other is a complex hip-rider that kind of wraps around and snuggles up to me. Both work well for me, and if I stand sideways to you, the angle the shoulder straps make with relationship to the long axis of my body is radically different from one pack to the other.

How do you test for fit and comfort when you're buying a pack?

Start by letting the outfitter fit the pack to you. The pack should be loaded with a weight approximating 20 percent of your body weight, which is the maximum you should carry if you plan to enjoy your time in the outback. Less is better; less is more. When you try on the pack, don't wear a belt, please. You can't carry a pack comfortably wearing a wide, stiff belt and a belt buckle that looks like you won the all-around cowboy award at the Fort Worth Stock Show. Wear comfortable pants that will lie flat under a backpack.

The pack must be comfortable. The frame, that is, must be comfortable. It must fit well, allow you reasonable freedom of movement, not cramp your arms or compress your chest, and must stay put when you walk. A pack that sways and meanders as you move is a pain in the neck until you get tired; then it becomes a hazard. The bag—the container for the things contained—is very nearly meaningless. The pack must fit. Period.

If I were pressed to choose one type of backpack for the beginning backpacker, I'd choose an external-frame pack (Figure 14) with a sturdy hipbelt and a packbag, divided top and bottom, that covers about ¾ of the length of the frame, so I have the option of carrying gear underneath it. I'd also like a top extension on the packframe, so I could carry gear lashed to that if I chose.

What? No internal-frame pack?

It's up to you. The internal-frame pack (Figure 15) is limited in terms of load distribution ability, and to a great extent it is designed for people who have determined their gear over the years and who use the internal-frame pack for specialty subsets within the sport. The relatively compact internal-frame bags are generally cut to permit considerable freedom of movement, so they're excellent for ski touring, bushwhacking, scrambling over rocks, and anything else requiring flexible strength. For straight-ahead backpacking, though, the external-frame pack is a functional, inexpensive option.

A note in passing. We're enamored, as a nation, with multipurpose gadgets. "Hey, folks, check it out! This pack is just perfect for backpacking, ski touring, rock climbing, canoeing, and taking your three-month-old to the supermarket so she can set a new world record by breaking thirty-seven jars of dill pickles with one sweep of her chubby little arm! Hurry, hurry, hurry! Check it out!"

Don't get trampled in the rush. There is no such thing as an all-purpose pack. If you camp on skis, get a pack designed for the job. If you canoe a lot, get a bespoke canoe pack. Otherwise, you'll go through five "all-purpose" packs before you give up in disgust and do it the right way, which is to have a pack for a function or for a closely related group of functions.

FIGURE 15
An internal-frame pack.
(Photo: Kelty)

Hints on Packing. You're best served if you keep the heavier items high in the pack and close to the back of the pack—the part that lies against the frame.

Here's how I do it (see Figure 16): The tent goes on top of the pack, lashed to the extension bar. The sleeping bag/sleeping pad, also in its stuff bag, goes on the frame under the packbag. If I had a full-length bag (which I don't like much), the sleeping gear would go into the big bottom compartment. As my packbag is divided, food and cookgear go in the top compartment, resting on top of whatever I choose to take along for warmth. That's usually a lightweight polypro shirt, polypro long johns (even in summer), and a lightweight fleece jacket. This area catches any extra clothing I might bring, too, such as a change of undershorts and socks. The stove and the fuel bottle go into side pockets, as does a water bottle and the water filter. The bottom compartment holds personal gear (I take a book and a notebook), a small first-aid kit put together after reading Dr. Bill Forgey's very comprehensive *Wilderness Medicine* (The Globe Pequot Press), an extra match safe, a flashlight, a knife, a stubby candle in a tin, and some stuff that comes under the heading of "health and beauty aids," like toothbrush, toothpaste, bug dope, sunscreen, reading glasses, lip salve, needle and thread, another match safe, and toilet paper, all in a small stuff

External- vs. internal-frame backpacks

	ADVANTANGES	DISADVANTAGES
External-frame	Inexpensive	Not as stable as
	Easier to organize gear	internal-frame
	Can carry heavier loads	Generally not as
	Can walk more upright on	comfortable
	smooth terrain	
Interal-frame	Comfortable	Can be more
	Provides excellent balance	expensive
	and stability	
	Easier to transport in a car	Less convenient
	or plane	access to
		some items

bag. A length of neatly reefed chute cord goes in here, too, for hanging up the food bag out of reach of critters.

I tend to be a "compartment freak." I like pockets in my packs (all but my canoe packs), and I like to keep items in stuff bags or heavy duty ziploc inside the pack. It keeps me from losing gear. It also lets me find things in a hurry, even in the dark. Why should I need to find things in the dark? Because I frequently walk in the dark, just as I frequently paddle in the dark. If you're going somewhere for a weekend, you can extend the useful time—time spent in the outback—by taking the first steps or strokes Friday night. And it raises an ordinary outing to the level of adventure as well. Things do go bump in the night out there. The person who says that the woods are quiet and peaceful ain't never been there, for sure!

Raingear stays under the pack flap, so it's easily accessible. Maps go into the header pocket on the pack flap. My compass goes into my shirt pocket. If I take a camera, I'll tether it to the packframe, where it's reasonably accessible. I don't usually take a camera except for "record shots," because I've never been able to shoot seriously on a pleasure trip. If I seek photographs, I go out just for photographs. When I lived in New York State, I wouldn't have considered taking binoculars. Here in Michigan, the jackpine and cutover terrain is swarming with birds. Alas, my binoculars are both bulky and heavy, so I saved the bucks I used to spend buying tobacco to put into a vest-pocket pair of binocs that will truly live in a pocket and be there when I want them. Hey, you don't get many chances in this life to see a Kirtland's warbler!

Some of this gear gets split up if my wife and I walk together. I'll slough off the tent poles on her, perhaps the cookpots, and some of the food. The idea is that no member of the party should be overburdened. I will not carry her little square foam pillow, although I'll gladly boost it in the wee small hours. I use my lightweight pile jacket in the sleeping bag stuff sack as a pillow.

How much should all of this weigh? I'd like to keep the weight at or under 20 percent of my body weight, which is about 165 pounds. This results in a pack of under 35 pounds, which is more than liveable. If

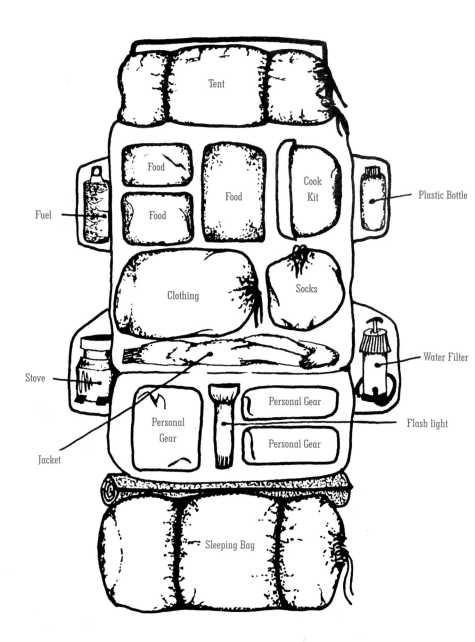

FIGURE 16

An example of a well-organized pack. Clothing should include extra socks, polypro T-shirt, and pants. Personal gear should include a book, medical kit, writing pad, matches (waterproofed), flashlight, emergency candles, and hygienic items.

FIGURE 17

Putting on a backpack:

a) Bend your knees and grab the shoulder straps;

b) Rest the pack on your knee; put your right arm through the shoulder strap and...

c) Swing it onto your back;

d) Put your left arm through the other shoulder strap;

e) Cinch the hipbelt and tighten the shoulder straps.

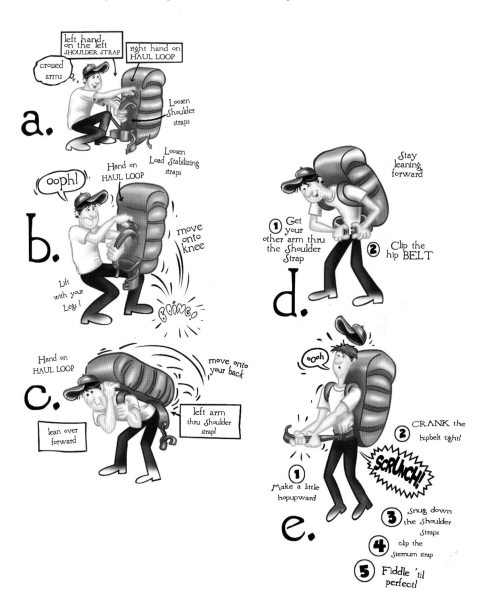

your pack fits, and you need to do it in an emergency, you can carry half your body weight with no problem, but with no fun either. The key to that kind of packing—and the key to lightweight packing as well—is how you get the pack on and off your back.

Load 'Em Up and Move 'Em Out. It's amazing what gets perpetrated on the unsuspecting pilgrim with a backpack. For example, the backpacking public has been solemnly told that the easiest way to "shoulder" your burden (you really "hip" your burden, of course) is to sit down, kind of wiggle into the packstraps, and then just roll forward and stand up. What a wonderful way to do in your back and get a hernia at the same time!

Here's how to get into harness with a loaded pack (see Figure 17): I'm right-handed. If you're a lefty, you may want to switch sides, but I'm not sure it really matters. Unlatch the hipbelt. Loosen both shoulder straps. Pick the pack up with your right hand on the crossbar from which the shoulder straps are suspended and your left hand on the right-hand strap ("right" as it would be as you are wearing it). Get the pack up high enough so you can support its weight mostly on your right knee. Now, slide your right arm and shoulder under the right-hand shoulder strap, using your knee to boost the weight up. Grab the shoulder strap with your right hand somewhere around where the padded area meets the nylon webbing, and keep the pack from pivoting with your elbow. (It's easier than it sounds.) Now, slip your left arm under the left-hand shoulder strap, roll your shoulders forward, and fasten the hip belt. Tighten the shoulder straps and begin the ritual dance of loosening and tightening, wriggling and jiggling, to get everything settled in. Easy! Your leg does the heavy work; your arms position things more than lift things.

To get out of the pack, loosen the left shoulder strap, slide out of it, and then release the hipbelt. The pack will still be pretty solidly positioned on your right shoulder. Reach across your body with your left hand, grab the right shoulder strap, and simply turn out from under the pack, which will slide down onto your knee, from whence it can be slid down to the ground. It works. Try it a few times in the living room until it becomes second nature. The time to learn it is not when you're tired!

CHAPTER 6

Woods-personship

There are always items that don't fit comfortably into neat categories. They're ways of seeing and ways of thinking rather than ways of doing, and sometimes they get lost or overlooked in the vast mass of "how-to." Let's chat about some of these things.

Basic Route Finding. This isn't a small textbook on map and compass work. For that, I cheerfully refer you to Cliff Jacobson's FalconGuide *Basic Illustrated Map & Compass*. Like all of Cliff's work, it's a model of clarity.

What I want to talk about with you is the simplest of all compass skills—one you'll use almost exclusively when you take a random scoot in the woods. It's called "walking a field bearing." You don't need a map for it, but you obviously need a compass. The best kind is mounted on a plate. It's sometimes called an orienteering compass (Figure 18), although an orienteering compass is a specialized version of the baseplate unit.

Here's the situation. You're out in the hilly country that starts about 12 miles inland from Lake Huron in the northern part of Michigan's lower peninsula. You recognize the terrain for what it is—big sand dunes that formed along the shores of a much older Lake Huron. The land's been burned over frequently, and while it's easy walking, the scrub oak and jackpine are pretty thick. And most jackpines look alike. You've left your car along the road, and you want to roam a little. Great! When faced with that kind of impulse, yield to it. Your life will be richer for it.

So you start, with your daypack and your compass. Before you go anywhere, point the direction-of-travel arrow at some prominent object in the direction toward which you're heading. It could be a distinctive tree or maybe just what seems to be a cleared area in a hundred yards or so. Now turn the dial of the compass—called

FIGURE 18

An orienteering compass.

(Photo: Johnson Outdoors, Inc./Silva)

the compass housing in formal parlance, should you ever have to speak to a compass—until the red end of the magnetic needle points toward zero degrees. Now read your field bearing at the index on the dial. Keep the magnetic needle framed inside the orienting arrow on the bottom of the compass housing as a quick check on your bearing.

Now start walking toward that first objective you sighted. When you get there, take another sighting along the bearing you've been walking, and walk to it. Simple, yes?

Well it's simple until you drop down off one hillock and stare at a neat little bog that you'd rather not cross because you might sink out of sight. Stop and look. Most little bogs are not punchbowls of stagnant water; they're small, dying lakes. There's an inlet and an outlet to this bog, and it should be no mystery to you that the inlet is on the "high" side of the bog. You're walking a bearing of 65 degrees already. Sight against some landmark and start walking. Take a moment to look back over your shoulder, though, to see where you were.

This time, count every double step you take, just like the Roman legionnaires did. In other words, every time your left foot strikes the ground, you count. Record the number of paces (remember your Latin?

Multi millia passuum?) in your little pocket notebook that always goes with you. When you arrive at the high side of the bog, turn left 90 degrees, and lo and behold, you're back at your familiar 65-degree field bearing. Walk this bearing for long enough to clear the far side of the bog (counting your paces, of course), and turn left again. Now you'll be walking a bearing of 65 degrees minus 90 degrees, or 345 degrees. (There are 360 degrees in a circle.) Sight your objective, and follow this bearing for the same number of paces you took back when you turned right to avoid the bog. After you've done that, you should be directly opposite where you started from when your detour began. Turn right, back to your 65-degree bearing, sight against another landmark, and start walking again.

You may have to detour around several things, even on a very casual ramble, but if you make your turns 90 degrees and keep track of your paces, you should be able to go into the bush for quite a while without a map and come back out again. You'll do this more easily if you take the time, at each turning and even when you're just walking that same old familiar bearing, to look around and familiarize yourself with the terrain. Don't look on this as a "survival skill" or any other sort of precious nonsense. You're out there to look around in the first place! Take the time to look, to see, in an unhurried fashion, and when you come back, the terrain will be familiar and friendly rather than foreboding and formidable.

Getting back is like getting out, but backwards. If we walked out at a field bearing of 65 degrees, we walk back at 65 plus 180, or 225 degrees. This is called a back bearing, and there's nothing at all mysterious about it.

However, you probably won't come out at exactly the same place on the road unless you've observed very carefully on the way in. You'll be close. In fact you'll probably be right on the money when you leave the first bog you encountered. But unless the road along which you left your car is pretty straight, chances are good that your car won't be in sight when you get out. This is no problem; it probably won't be over a quarter-mile off—but in what direction?

Here's what you do. When you arrive at that last known point, which in this case is the bog, cheat a little if you can't visualize the terrain exactly. Instead of walking out at 225 degrees, walk out at 230 degrees. You know that you won't wind up at your car, but you're sure to wind up a bit west of the car. Turn left, and your car will be there, just around the bend.

Simple, yes? Yes! And simpler still if you take the time to look around—which is why you're out there in the first place.

Zero Impact. Okay folks, we need to face the facts. There are far too many people on this planet and far too little woods for every person to wreak havoc wherever they choose. We must be responsible for what we do out there, and believe me, everything we do makes a difference.

Zero impact basics

1. Stay on the trail. That means don't cut switchbacks and don't widen the trail by walking around muddy sections. Your boots will dry; the vegetation you trample may not grow back.

2. Camp at an established campsite. There is no need to flatten a wildflower meadow when there is a flat bed of pine needles. Also, there is no point in altering the site by digging trenches, chopping down bushes, or cutting tree limbs. Work with what you've got, and use your head, not your knife.

3. Pack it in, pack it out. It's that simple.

4. Never put soap in a lake or stream. Even biodegradable soap does not degrade in water. Scatter soapy water (from washing dishes, clothes, and yourself) at least 200 feet from the source.

5. The same goes for human waste. Go at least 200 feet from water and from your camp. Dig a hole 4 to 8 inches deep, do your business, take a stick and mix the waste with soil so the bacteria can get straight to work, then cover the hole. And please, pack out toilet paper. There are few things more disgusting than finding a bunch of catholes with toilet paper hanging out of them. Carry an extra ziploc for used toilet paper. Better yet, don't use toilet paper at all! Gross, you say? No! Be creative; leaves, soft pinecones, (make sure you wipe in the right direction!), and snow are all good substitutes—and you don't have to bother with packing them out.

6. Use a camp stove, not a campfire.

7. Leave everything as you found it. There should be no impact of your presence. And all the feathers, rocks, leaves, skulls, etc., need to stay in the woods. Take pictures, take memories, but don't take the deer antlers to put on your mantle. They are better off where they are, thank you.

Knives. Carry a pocket knife or a small sheath knife. You don't need a "survival knife" or any such stuff, because except for making a fuzz stick to start a fire on a wet day, the most dangerous thing you'll be stabbing is commercial peanut butter.

Staying Found. Staying found is an attitude as well as a skill, and more people get lost on a casual walk than on long trips. Why? The long trips are generally well-planned. You're going with maps, and you're paying attention to them. Your map and compass skills are well-honed, and because this is a Big Trip, you're paying attention to your surroundings. That's the key. Take the time to turn around and see where you've been. Take the time to notice where the sun is as you walk. Be aware of your surroundings. You might not know exactly where you are, but you know where you came from. And that's all you need to know.

Leadership. Most backpackers rarely find themselves in a position where they're on a trip that requires formal leadership, so we won't talk about that. But any trip of any length with one other person is a leadership situation, or at least a situation in which decisions have to be made. Guard against certain things, please. Do not EVER press people beyond their capacities in a recreational situation. That's not "getting tough"; that's getting clinically sadistic. Do not let recreational walks turn into situations that require a life-or-death effort by sheer carelessness or lack of observation. If you're soaked to the skin and shivering, don't press on. Make camp there, eat, and get warm before you settle into hypothermia. And if one person shows signs of fatigue, hypothermia, or heat stroke, don't insist on toughing it out. Make camp or, if on a day hike, take care of the problem NOW before you have a full-blown emergency on your hands.

Walking with Kids and the Elderly. This is a leadership function that isn't nearly as heroic as you might envision in your fantasies, but it is probably the most important leadership function you'll ever exercise.

Kids and Gray Panthers are interested in the here and now, and singularly uninterested in goals. I wanted to soak it all up when I was a kid, and in my advanced years I want to soak it all up because I might not travel this way again. When I was a younger man, though, the challenge was getting there, usually in a heck of a hurry. Hey, I had all of my life to putter around and smell the flowers!

So, if you walk with children or the elderly, you will walk to the beat of a different drummer. You can relax and remember how it was when you were a kid. Or you can unwind and listen while Dad or Grandpa points out the difference between Pinus banksiana and Pinus resinosa to you for the twentieth time. But this time, maybe, it'll stick, and you can tell your kids someday.

A walk in the woods with the old and the young is a walk with no objective beyond the pleasure of the moment. There is no challenge to overcome, because a fringed gentian only offers beauty. And there is nothing at all to conquer except your own addiction to conquering.

Bring something special for lunch. Bring the bird book. Bring the wildflower book. Bring the binoculars. And bring an easy mind, secure and happy in the knowledge that this is not YOUR trip. It belongs to somebody else for whom you care very much. And if you don't get to that neat pond three ridges over, you'll probably get to somewhere you never knew existed until you saw it through eyes wiser than yours.

Enjoy.

Final Chortle. Smell the roses. Enjoy the view. Be kind to your companions and to the world you walk through. And if you see a fellow backpacker in the woods, be sure to wave!

Appendix:
Equipment Lists

Annotated Equipment List for a day trip

1. Small pack. I prefer a compartmentalized daypack for convenience.
2. Comfortable shoes or boots. Size them to fit a pair of heavy wool socks and lightweight liner socks.
3. Lightweight rain jacket with hood. The mostly waterproof/breathable fabrics work well.
4. Water bottle. Take a liter. Yes, it's heavy. You'll never notice the weight. Wrap it up in the rainshell to keep it cool.
5. Munchies. A hard roll, some cheese, and a few peanuts are well nigh perfect for me. It may not be for you. For a few hours in the woods, food is more of a consolation than a necessity. A pocket knife is part of the food pack.
6. Map and compass. Even if you don't need it, view it as a data bank and as a creator of enthusiasm for future walks. Also, the time to learn map and compass work is when you don't need to know it.
7. First-aid kit. I honor this more in the abeyance, but a small kit and an ankle wrap are the way to fly. Keep both in your pack all the time, and you'll never leave them at home. Iodine tabs go in the kit.
8. Insect repellent and sunscreen. Keep them in your pack.
9. Field guides, notebook, and pen. Your choice. We always have a bird guide, a wildflower guide, and a pair of binoculars with us and frequently a tree guide as well, if we're out of familiar territory.
10. Toilet paper.

This is a very basic list. I have no doubt that most authorities would say that my safety equipment is very sparse, and no doubt it is. This is for a short jaunt in easy country. If you're walking in more rugged terrain, or in a trackless area, or in marginal weather, you might well augment this list with a lightweight fleece jacket or polypro sweater, matches in a waterproof container, a space blanket, and lightweight rain pants or rain chaps.

By now you've outgrown your small pack, so take the backpack off the wall (it has its own first-aid kit, remember?) and be comfortable. If there's snow on the ground, beef up your footgear, take an extra pair of socks with you, staple your sunglasses to your ears, grab your shell mittens with wool mitten liners, and enjoy, enjoy, enjoy.

An Annotated Equipment List for Overnighting

1. Frame backpack. Check all attachment points, rub the zippers with a candle, shake out the mice.

2. Tent. When was the last time the seams were sealed? Best do it now, because you can't do it at two in the morning when the wind is wailing and the rain is falling so hard it smokes. And you will check the poles and tent stakes, of course. Good!

3. Sleeping system. Sleeping bag, pillow if you need one, and a sleeping pad. I don't go out there to rough it; I carry a Therm-A-Rest and laugh at the small extra weight.

4. Boots. If you're carrying your house on your back, you'll need something sturdier on your feet than tennis or running shoes. The rule's the same: heavy socks and liner socks.

5. Cooking gear. A small stove, a couple of pots, a pot lifter, a scrub pad and biodegradable soap, a tablespoon (all-purpose, for eating and mixing), and a cup. All the cookgear is clean, of course, and in its own stuff sack. And the stove has been checked over, and you packed the fuel in its own pack pocket? Of course! And you did throw in the little plastic bag of absolutely necessary stove parts?

6. Food. Your choice. I keep it simple, preferring to eat to live rather than live to eat, but I always take along something sinfully self-indulgent. Take enough for an extra day—and never assume you'll catch fish!

7. Water filter. The alternative has most unpleasant names: turistas, Montezuma's Revenge, the trots.

8. Other stuff you'd take on an overnight trip. Of course you'll take the usual, like the first-aid kit, survival kit, the ankle wrap, the pocket knife, the map, the compass, clothing to suit the weather, personal medication, and such. What you need to think about is how much other stuff to take. You may want to trade the field guides for a small camera, or you may prefer to take all of them. You'll certainly take your liter water bottle, and you may want another one for convenience in cooking. I do. Sometimes I fill both and tote them along if I'm in "new" country, because I don't know where the water supplies are. And I won't overburden myself with a lot of extra clothes. Pounds for warmth and dryness; not an ounce for vanity. You can survive without a change of clothes for a weekend.

9. Flashlight. Candle lanterns are neat toys, and I usually take one, but a small flashlight (spare bulb inside) is the preferred working tool. The batteries are fresh, of course.

10. A relaxed mind. Roll with the punches, enjoy the rain.

Index

About the Author and Editor

Harry Roberts was the editor of *Canoesports Journal* and an avid outdoorsman, canoeist, hiker, and camper.

Russ Schneider has been a backpacking, rafting, and fishing guide with Glacier Wilderness Guide since 1993 and has edited many how-to FalconGuides. His books include *Backpacking Tips*, *Best Hikes Along the Continental Divide*, *Fishing Glacier National Park*, and *Hiking the Columbia River Gorge*.

Visit the premiere outdoor online community

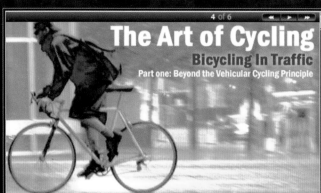

FALCON GUIDES®

LOGIN | CREATE AN ACCOUNT

Search

HOME   ABOUT US   CONTACT US   BOOKS   BLOGS   PHOTOS   TRAIL FINDER

4 of 6   ◄ ► ►►

The Art of Cycling
Bicycling In Traffic
Part one: Beyond the Vehicular Cycling Principle

HIKING WITH KIDS

HAPPY TRAILS Hiking in the Great Outdoors is a simple gift we all can give our children, grandchildren, and young friends. Unlike playing music, writing poetry, painting pictures, or other activities that also can fill your soul, hiking does not require any special skill. All you need to do is put one foot in front of the other in the outdoors, repeatedly. And breathe deeply.

○ **LEARN MORE**

■ FEATURED NEW BOOK

SCAVENGER HIKE ADVENTURES: GREAT SMOKY MOUNTAINS NATIONAL PARK

A Totally New Interactive Hiking Guide

Introducing a brand new genre of hiking guide. Readers follow clues to find over 200 hidden natural and historic treasures on as many as 14 easy, moderate, and extreme hikes national parks. Follow the clues and find such things as a tree clawed open by a bear searching for food, an ancient Indian footpath, the remains of an old Model T Ford deep in the forest, and over 200 other unusual treasures.

○ CLICK HERE TO FIND OUT MORE

■ RECENT BLOG POSTS

○ A Dry River
○ Stat-mongering -- Look Out!
○ Lizard Man
○ Tropical Tip of Texas
○ Lions And Snakes and Bears...Oh My! "Don's PCT Update"
○ Bikin' in C'ville
○ The Red Store
○ Journey to Idyllwild
○ A Spring Quandary
○ Whew!! Rocky Mountain book is printed I'm going camping!!

more

■ EXPERT BLOGS

○ Arrowleaf Balsamroot—Another
By: Bert Gildart
○ Splitter camps #2
By: Katie Brown
○ Splitter camp
By: Katie Brown
○ Alaska Boating Adventure

outfit your mind

Chris Sharma
• Beth Rodden
• Dean Potter
• Jason Kehl
• Josh Wharton
• Steph Davis

falcon.com